NATALIE BAKER

Christmas Piano
for Beginner

The Best Collection
of the Most Popular Christmas Songs
at Easy and Intermediate Levels.

How to listen to audio:
It is possible to listen or download all the mp3 audio tracks by accessing the following link:
https://urly.it/3qj8b
or by scanning the QR Code:

Layout: Mauro Costa

INDEX

O Come O Come Emmanuel

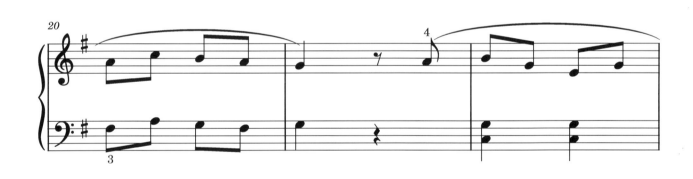

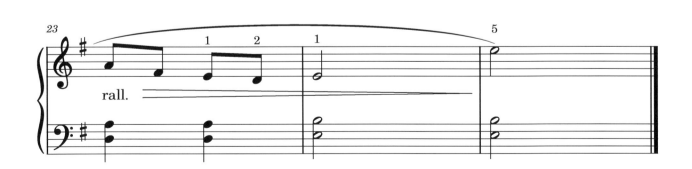

O Little Town of Bethlehem

O Christmas Tree

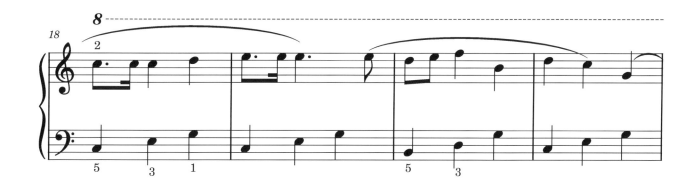

Deck the Hall ✓

15/12/22

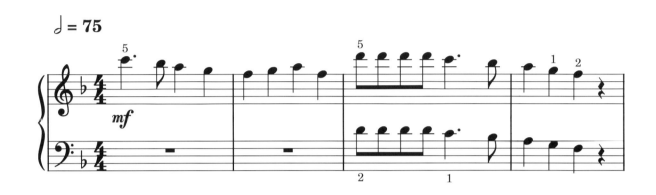

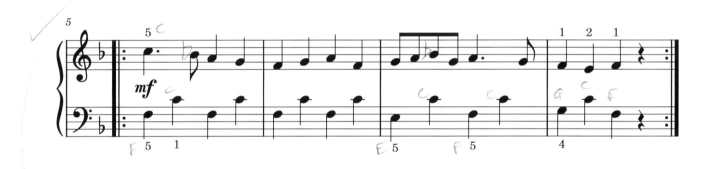

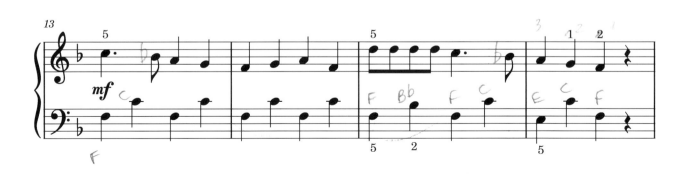

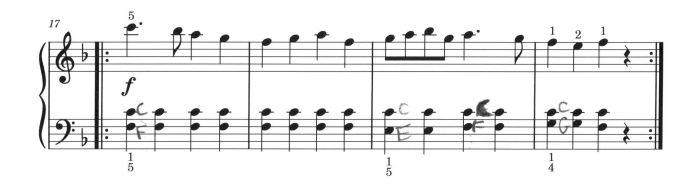

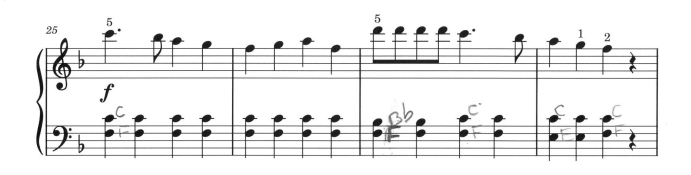

Jingle Bells

13

What Child is This
(Greensleeves)

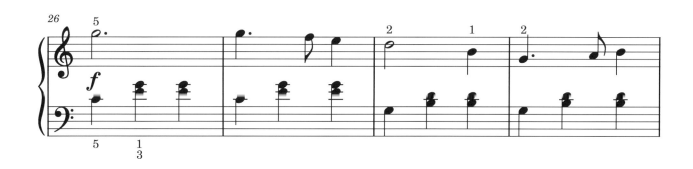

15

We Three Kings

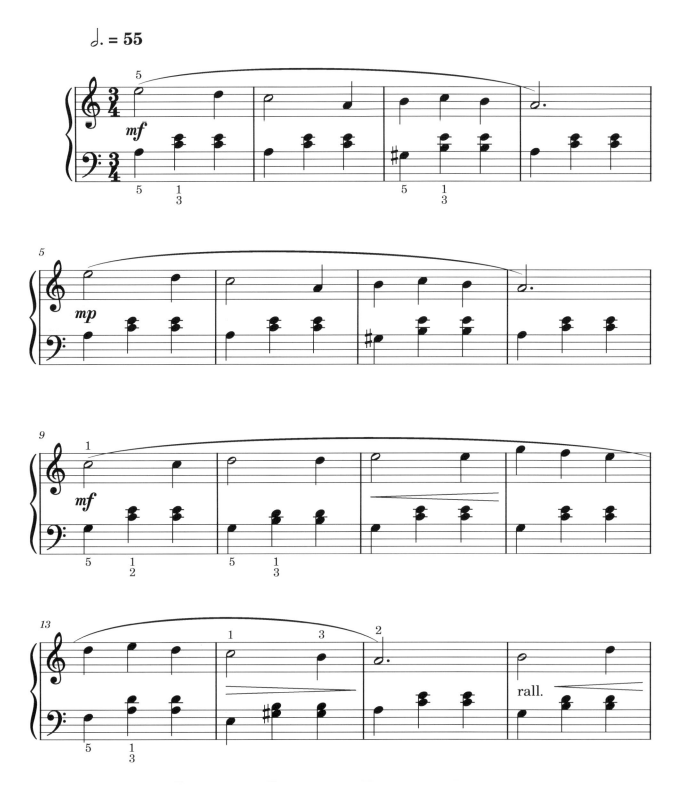

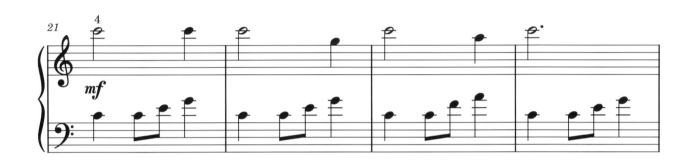

Oh Holy Night

19

Silent Night

Hark! The Herald Angels Sing

Come, Thou Long-Expected Jesus

The First Noel

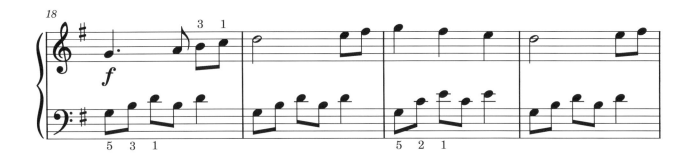

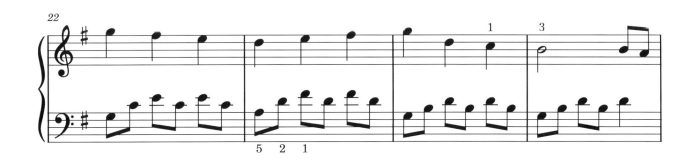

I Saw Three Ships

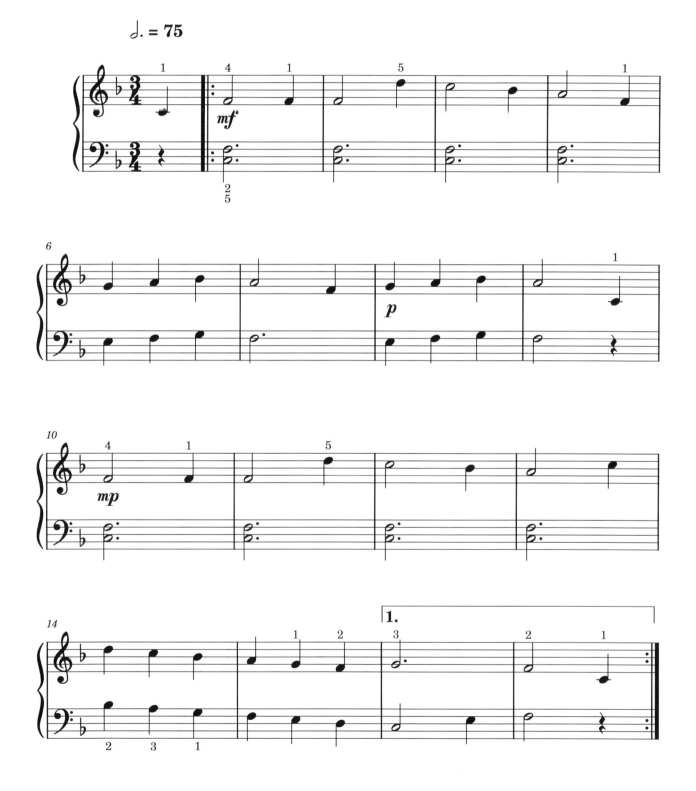

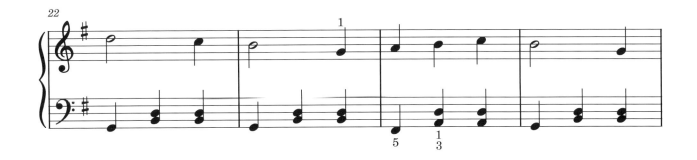

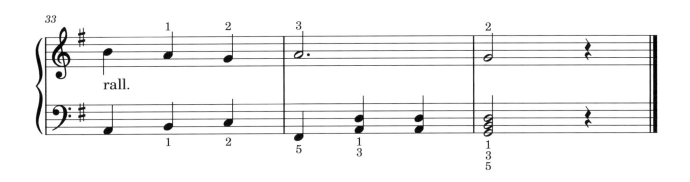

Auld Lang Syne

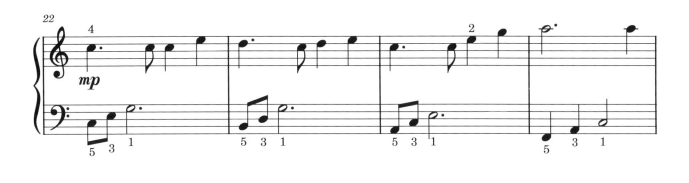

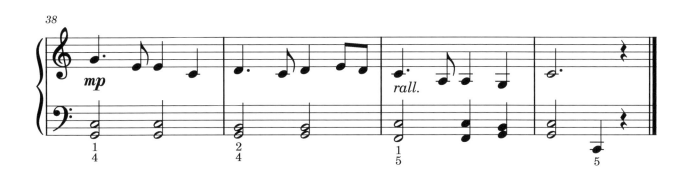

Ding Dong Merrily on High

Angels We Have Heard on High

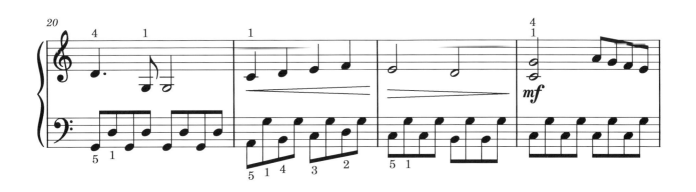

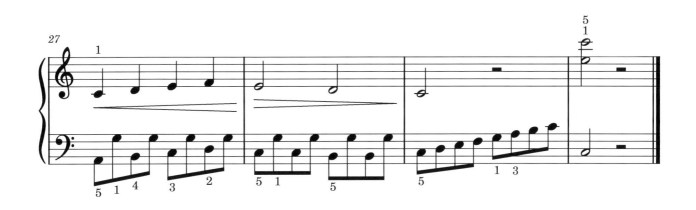

We Wish You a Merry Christmas ✓

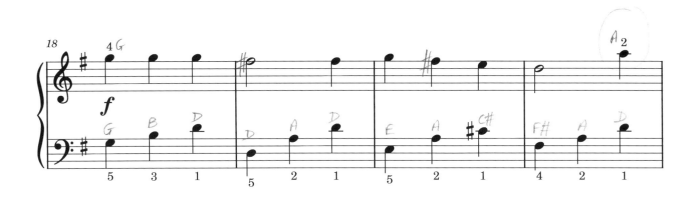

Joy to the World

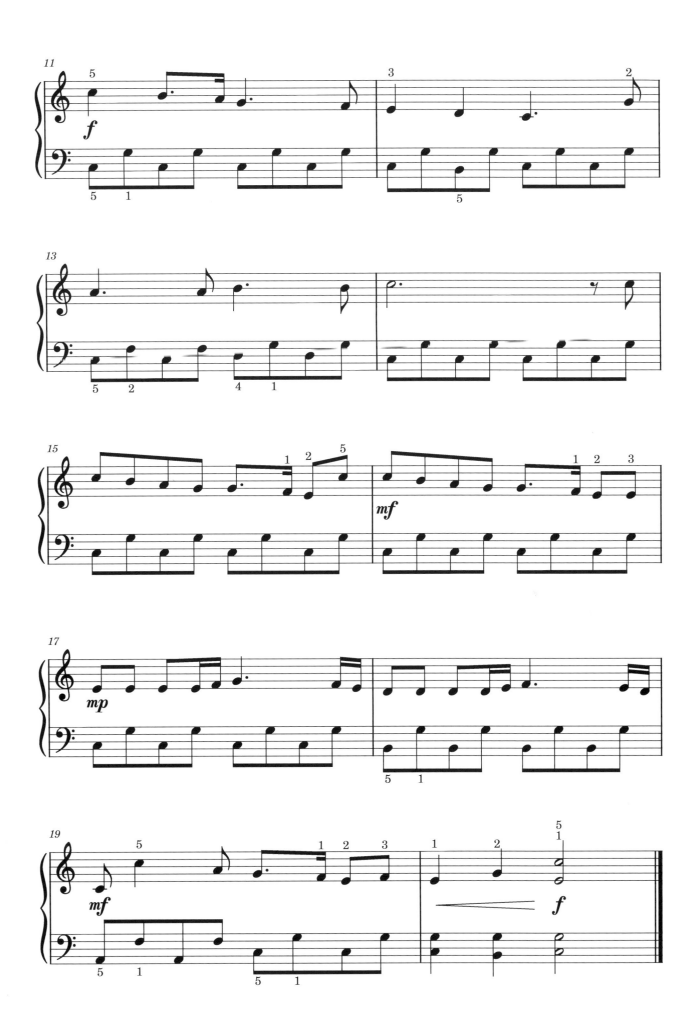

Oh Come All Ye Faithful

Printed in Great Britain
by Amazon

12310004R00025